REAL-LIFE MONSTERS
CREATURES
OF THE
RAIN FOREST

THE WORLD'S
WEIRDEST
RAIN FOREST
CREATURES

Thanks to the creative team:
Senior Editor: Alice Peebles
Designer: Lauren Woods and collaborate agency

Original edition copyright 2015 by Hungry Tomato Ltd.

Copyright © 2016 by Lerner Publishing Group, Inc.

Hungry Tomato™ is a trademark of
Lerner Publishing Group, Inc.

Hungry Tomato™
A division of Lerner Publishing Group, Inc.
241 First Avenue North
Minneapolis, MN 55401 USA

For reading levels and more information, look up this title at www.lernerbooks.com.

Main body text set in Century Gothic Regular 9.5/11.5
Typeface provided by Monotype Corporation

Library of Congress Cataloging-in-Publication Data

The Cataloging-in-Publication Data for *Creatures of the Rain Forest* is on file at the Library of Congress.

ISBN 978-1-4677-6363-9 (lib. bdg.)
ISBN 978-1-4677-7644-8 (pbk.)
ISBN 978-1-4677-7228-0 (EB pdf)

Manufactured in the United States of America
1 – VP – 7/15/15

REAL-LIFE MONSTERS
CREATURES
OF THE
RAIN FOREST

By Matthew Rake

Illustrated by Simon Mendez

HUNGRY
TOMATO™
Minneapolis

CONTENTS

RAIN FOREST MONSTERS

Rain forests are teeming with life, from big cats and majestic eagles to tiny insects that skitter across branches and the forest floor. Rain forests cover less than two percent of the earth's surface near the equator—yet more than 50 percent of the world's living things are squeezed inside them.

And they are home to some of the weirdest, most wonderful, and downright dangerous animals on Earth.

Some of the smallest creatures are the deadliest. Take the poison dart frog. It's a beautiful, brilliantly colored little amphibian, but it has enough poison to kill a couple of elephants! The Brazilian wandering spider is almost as poisonous. It likes to live in banana plants—so watch out next time you pick up a bunch of bananas at the supermarket.

There's no escape from rain forest monsters in the water. There, you'll find the goliath tigerfish, possibly the world's fiercest freshwater fish. The green anaconda likes to lurk in the water, too. It's 30 feet (9 meters) of pure muscle, and it uses it immense strength to crush, suffocate, or drown its prey. Then there's the electric eel, which swims around firing electrical charges at anything it wants to eat. It really is a fish with a superpower.

Meanwhile, keep an eye on the skies. The harpy eagle rules over the rain forest. It sits like a monarch, high up on a branch, until it sees a nice sloth or monkey to pluck from the trees. The vampire bat, just as you would expect from its name, comes out only at night to drink the blood of sleeping animals. And, sorry, but these animals sometimes include humans!

So if you want to find out more about the strange, scary, and truly shocking creatures of the rain forest, read on. It's a jungle out there.

Length: 0.2–0.3 inches (4.6–7.5 mm)
Weight: less than 0.04 ounces (1 g)
Location: northern South America

There are about 3,200 species of treehopper. This creature sucks up plant sap through a strawlike mouth. Most species inhabit the rain forests of tropical countries, but some live on every continent (except Antarctica).

What makes treehoppers completely different from other insects is the bizarrely shaped growths that emerge from their bodies. This growth is a pronotum, or external structure, often called a helmet, and each species has its own style. Many are magnificently elaborate and look like works of modern art. Check out this Brazilian treehopper (*right*). Those four hairy bulbs are not its eyes or antennae. They're its helmet.

PUTTING OFF PREDATORS?

Some scientists used to think the purpose of the helmet was to attract a mate, as peacock feathers or deer antlers do. In some treehopper species, the males have different helmets from the females—but both male and female Brazilian treehoppers have the same hairy-bulb helmets. So scientists think these bulbs may deter predators. To birds, the bulbs probably appear poisonous or dangerous. Certainly the helmets of other treehoppers are designed to keep predators away. Some helmets look exactly like dangerous ants or wasps. Others are horned or horseshoe-shaped to make the treehopper look fearsome. Still others have spiky thorns and bright colors to warn predators that the bug is definitely not going to be a tasty snack. Several helmets look exactly like leaves, twigs, or bark so predators don't see the treehopper underneath.

SIZE

1

POWER

1

STRENGTH

1

AGGRESSION

1

DEADLINESS

1

TOTAL

5

TOTALLY
TOXIC
POISON DART FROG

Length: 0.59 – 2.4 in (1.5 – 6 cm)
Weight: 1 oz (28 g)
Location: northern South America
and southern Central America

Poison dart frogs are among the most brilliant and beautiful animals on Earth. But they don't look pretty to predators—far from it. Their wonderful colors and designs have one purpose: to warn carnivores that this animal is very dangerous. Since the poison is actually on the frog's skin, it's definitely a case of "look but don't touch!"

DEATH BY PARALYSIS

The golden dart frog is the most lethal of all the dart frogs. Packed into this matchbox-sized amphibian is enough poison to kill an army of 10,000 mice, 10 to 20 humans, or a couple of elephants. The poison attacks the nervous system, stopping it from sending signals to the muscles. The result is almost instant paralysis. The snake *Liophis epinephelus* is the only known predator of this frog—it's immune to the toxins.

MAKING A BLOWGUN

In Colombia, people use the poison from golden dart frogs to help them hunt monkeys and birds. They hold the frog on a wooden spear over a fire until its skin blisters and bubbles of poison form. They coat their darts with this poison—it can keep its deadly effect for more than two years.

The blowgun is made from a hollowed-out piece of wood, sometimes more than 6.5 feet (2 m) long. The user aims at the animal and then blows. The darts are usually kept in a bamboo quiver to prevent accidents!

SIZE

2

POWER

2

STRENGTH

2

AGGRESSION

1

DEADLINESS

10

TOTAL

17

8 PURE POISON

BRAZILIAN WANDERING SPIDER

Length: 6 in (15 cm) including legs
Weight: about 4 oz (110 g)
Location: South America and southern Central America

Its Latin name, Phoneutria, means "murderess," and you can see why. It's huge, can be very aggressive, and, according to Guinness World Records, is the most poisonous spider in the world. Its bite is 30 times deadlier than a rattlesnake's. All in all, this spider is not good news for anyone who comes in contact with it.

JUNGLE CREEPERS

Wandering spiders got their name because they travel the jungle floor at night, rather than living in a burrow or a web. They look for prey such as crickets, praying mantises, and scorpions. They also look for larger animals, including tree frogs, mice, and lizards.

STOWAWAY SPIDERS

When threatened, the wandering spider will raise its two forelegs and expose its large red jaws. During the day, wandering spiders seek cover in termite mounds or under fallen logs and rocks. They often turn up in people's houses, looking for dark places in clothes, boots, boxes and log piles. Another favorite hiding place is banana plants, and sometimes they travel across oceans and continents in boxes of the fruit. In 2005, a chef in the United Kingdom was bitten by a stowaway wandering spider. He took a picture of it on his phone before passing out. The doctors treating him sent the picture to experts at nearby Bristol Zoo, who identified the spider, so the doctors knew what antivenom to use. The man survived.

SIZE

4

POWER

3

STRENGTH

3

AGGRESSION

4

DEADLINESS

9

TOTAL

23

7 IRON STRENGTH
HERCULES BEETLE

Length: 1.5 – 6.7 in (4 – 17 cm)
Weight: 0.41 – 1.32 oz (11.5 – 37.5 g)
Location: Central and South America

BIG EATER

The Hercules beetle uses its strength to forage among heavy branches and stones in the undergrowth while looking for its favorite food: rotting fruit buried in the soil. This creature certainly has a hearty appetite—in a laboratory, a Hercules beetle was seen feeding for 24 hours nonstop.

So who is the true strongman of the animal kingdom? A lion? An elephant? How about the Hercules beetle? Yes, it is only the size of a matchbox, but it can carry 850 times its own weight. That's the equivalent of the average human lifting 50 compact cars. No wonder this beetle was named after the Greek hero Hercules, who had legendary strength.

SIZE
4

POWER
6

STRENGTH
9

AGGRESSION
4

DEADLINESS
1

TOTAL
24

BEETLE BATTLES

The male Hercules beetle has two horns: one on top of its head, curving up, and the other emerging from its body, curving down. It can move its head horn up so the two horns can operate together like pincers.

Some scientists think the horns are used in defense, although experts have not seen the Hercules beetle being attacked in the wild. The horns certainly come in handy when the males fight for females. These can be long battles.

The two males attempt to clasp and overpower each other with their horns. When one is successful, it uses its horns to lift and fling its opponent down.

6 FLYING
BLOODSUCKER
COMMON VAMPIRE BAT

Length: 3.5 in (9 cm)
Weight: 2 oz (57 g)
Location: Central and South America

You've heard of carnivores and herbivores, but what about sanguinivores? They are animals such as mosquitoes and leeches whose diet consists solely of blood. Only one mammal is a sanguinivore—meet the vampire bat.

1 During the darkest hours of the night, while most animals are asleep, the common vampire bat emerges from caves and tree hollows. It flies around in search of blood. When it finds a horse, cow, pig, or sometimes even a human, it lands nearby and creeps up on its victim.

2 Most bats are pretty helpless on the ground, but the vampire bat is very nimble. It quietly hops up on its prey and uses heat sensors in its nose to find the juiciest blood vessels. If the prey has hair, the bat shaves it with its canine and cheek teeth.

3 Then the bat uses its super-sharp incisor teeth to make a small, deep cut. The bite is relatively painless and rarely wakes a sleeping victim. The bat doesn't actually suck the blood but laps it up. And it has chemicals in its saliva to stop the blood from clotting while it drinks.

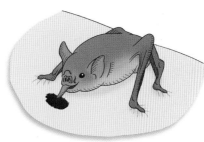

LIGHTENING ITS LOAD

The common vampire bat can consume at least half its body weight in one feed. The only problem is taking off again. Almost immediately after it begins to feed, it urinates to lighten its load! This means its victim not only has its blood sucked but gets peed on too!

SIZE	3
POWER	4
STRENGTH	5
AGGRESSION	8
DEADLINESS	6
TOTAL	26

HAIRY HORROR

GOLIATH BIRD-EATING SPIDER

Length: 11 in (28 cm) including legs
Weight: up to 6.2 oz (175 g)
Location: northeastern South America

This tarantula is definitely not to be messed with. It's the biggest spider in the world, and a large one will stretch over the edges of your dinner plate. Its fangs alone are 1 inch (2.5 centimeters) long, and they deliver a powerful venom.

The tarantula is also quick, nervous, and easily angered. If threatened, it makes a hissing noise by rubbing the bristles on its legs. If this doesn't do the trick, it flicks harpoon-shaped hairs at its enemy. It does this by rubbing its hind legs on its abdomen. Although small, these hairs can do serious harm to attackers, especially if they get into delicate areas such as the eyes or the mouth.

ATTACK ANYTHING!

This tarantula may be called a bird-eating spider, but it will attack virtually anything it meets. It generally hunts through the leaves on the forest floor, where it eats frogs, insects, lizards, snakes, earthworms, and small mammals such as mice. If it finds a bird's nest, it may kill the parents and chicks or puncture and drink the eggs. It attacks by stealth, sneaking up on its prey, before pouncing and overwhelming the unsuspecting victim. Then it inflicts its fatal toxic bite with its huge venom-filled fangs.

A TASTY TREAT OF TARANTULA

The bird-eating spider is a delicacy to some people in South America. They first singe off the harpoon-shaped hairs, then roast the spider in banana leaves. The white muscle meat tastes like smoky shrimp, while the gooey abdomen is gritty and bitter. After the meal, diners use the fangs as toothpicks to remove the spider's hard outer cuticle from their teeth. When was the last time your dinner came with built-in toothpicks?

SIZE

5

POWER

4

STRENGTH

5

AGGRESSION

8

DEADLINESS

5

TOTAL

27

Length: about 5 ft (1.5 m)
Weight: Up to 110 lb (50 kg)
Location: Central Africa

The Congo River runs through the rain forest in central Africa. It is not as long as the Amazon but is deeper and can be just as turbulent. Here, in the river's strongest currents, the goliath tigerfish likes to swim. With powerful muscles and a broad, tuna-like tail, it's able to navigate these waters easily, so catching a struggling fish is no problem.

Then the goliath tigerfish's 32 interlocking, viciously sharp teeth come into play. Each one is up to 1 inch (2.5 cm) long and can make a clean, almost surgical cut into the victim. These fish make the Amazon's piranhas look like cuddly cats.

SIZE
6

POWER
8

STRENGTH
8

AGGRESSION
8

DEADLINESS
6

TOTAL
36

FIERCEST FRESHWATER FISH

Producer Jeremy Wade, who made a TV documentary series called *River Monsters*, declared that his ultimate river monster is the goliath tigerfish. In his opinion, it is the most difficult freshwater fish to catch. After 25 years of visiting the Republic of the Congo, he finally caught a 78-pound (35-kilogram) specimen, but not without a struggle. To interest the tigerfish, Wade used a sizeable catfish as bait, but the tigerfish would bite off the catfish's rear half or underside. So Wade decided to try a multi-barbed book. Then guess what happened? That's right—the tigerfish wouldn't bite. This is a fish with brains as well as brawn. Finally, Wade hooked one, and despite some frantic head thrashing by the tigerfish, he landed it with the help of a friend wielding a net.

3 A REALLY SHOCKING FISH

ELECTRIC EEL

Length: 8 ft (2.5 m)
Weight: 44 lb (20 kg)
Location: northern South America

Electric eels live in the murky streams and lakes around the Amazon and Orinoco rivers, feeding on fish and sometimes amphibians, birds, and even small mammals.

To capture their prey, they have a superpower: electricity. Yes, they fire electric shocks through the water. One shock has enough power to knock a horse off its feet. Humans have reportedly been killed by electric eels—not outright, but because they have drowned after being been stunned.

MAKING AN IMPACT

The eel uses its electricity in three ways. It sends out small, 10-volt bursts to sense objects in the water. It also sends out stronger double or triple pulses, known as doublets or triplets, when searching for hidden prey. This makes the fish's muscles jerk, causing it to "jump" into the open.

The eel also has killer shocks—volleys of high-voltage pulses for capturing prey or defending itself from attack.

SIZE

7

POWER

7

STRENGTH

6

AGGRESSION

8

DEADLINESS

9

TOTAL

37

THE BIG SQUEEZE

GREEN ANACONDA

Length: 20 – 30 ft (6-9 m)
Weight: up to 500 lb (227 kg)
Location: northern South America

Anacondas live in the swamps and streams of the rain forests. They are sluggish on land but sleek and stealthy movers in the water. Like crocodiles, they have eyes and nostrils on top of their heads, so they can wait for prey while almost completely submerged.

They prey on fish, turtles, and caimans (a type of crocodile)—and swiftly slide out of the water to catch a wild pig, deer, capybara, or bird. Sometimes they go for jaguars too, although they often come out second best in that encounter. They will even eat each other. Since the female is larger, she usually eats the male.

CRUSHED, SUFFOCATED, OR DROWNED

The anaconda has no need for venom. To kill, it first locks its jaws onto its prey. It has six rows of teeth to do this—four rows of backward-pointing teeth in its top jaw and two rows in its bottom jaw. Then the anaconda coils its muscular body around the prey and squeezes until the prey is crushed or suffocated. The anaconda may drag a land animal into the water and drown it before consuming the carcass whole.

RAT CATCHER

Capybaras *(below left)* are the world's largest rodents and typically weigh 110 pounds (50 kg). They spend a lot of time in swamps, where they feed on the plants that grow there. However, this is also where the anaconda lurks. And with its green and brown markings, the anaconda is perfectly camouflaged, ready to launch a surprise attack . . .

SIZE	9
POWER	8
STRENGTH	9
AGGRESSION	8
DEADLINESS	8
TOTAL	42

1 APEX PREDATOR

HARPY EAGLE

Length: about 3.3 ft (1 m)
Weight: up to 20 lb (9 kg)
Location: Central and South America

Among the predators of the rain forest, harpy eagles are at the top of the food chain. Nothing eats harpies, but they will eat all sorts of other animals. Their favorite meals are sloths and monkeys, which they snatch from trees.

SUPERSIZED TALONS

You can discover a lot about a bird of prey by looking at its feet—and the harpy clearly eats big prey. Its legs are the same width as a child's wrist and its talons are the longest of any living eagle's. They measure up to 5 inches (13 cm)—that's the same size as a grizzly bear's. With these deadly talons, a harpy can exert amazing pressure, instantly crushing the bones of large mammals.

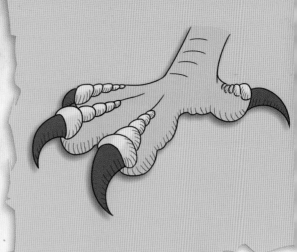

PATIENCE AND POWER

Harpies are huge birds—among other eagles, only the Steller's sea eagle and the Philippine eagle come close in size. As a result, it doesn't waste energy soaring over a rain forest. Instead, it perches on branches and scans the trees and ground for meals. Like all eagles, it has excellent eyesight. It can see objects less than 0.8 inches (2 cm) in size from almost 656 feet (200 m). And it apparently has endless patience—one harpy was observed waiting for 23 hours on a branch.

Once it sees its kill, the harpy is quick and decisive. It swoops down at speeds of up to 50 miles per hour (80 km/h) and snatches its prey with outstretched feet. It has a shorter wingspan than other big eagles, so it can move through the forest with ease.

QUICK KILL

The harpy kills prey with its fearsome talons, then rips off flesh with its razor-sharp beak. It usually take its prey back to the nest, but with big animals, it might eat what it can on a stump or a low branch.

SIZE	7
POWER	9
STRENGTH	9
AGGRESSION	9
DEADLINESS	9
TOTAL	43

ROGUES' GALLERY

TREEHOPPER

To keep predators away, some treehoppers have helmets that look like yucky animal droppings. Others have helmets that appears to be fungus oozing from their bodies so they look diseased.

POISON DART FROG

Scientists are unsure how poison dart frogs became so toxic. When raised in captivity, they don't develop poison. It's possible that they take in plant poisons, carried by the animals they eat in the wild, such as ants, termites, and beetles.

COMMON VAMPIRE BAT

The common vampire bat sometimes attacks humans—and carries diseases such as rabies. In 2010, more than 500 people of the Awajun tribe, from the Amazon region of Peru, had their blood sucked by vampire bats, and four of them died.

GOLIATH BIRD-EATING SPIDER

The bird-eating spider rarely eats birds, so how did it gets its name? Thank the German naturalist Maria Sibylla Merian, one of the few women scientists of the 17th and 18th centuries. From 1699 to 1701, she traveled around South America, where she drew the spider eating a hummingbird.

GREEN ANACONDA

Like other snakes, the anaconda's jaws are not fused together, which allows it to eat prey much bigger than its head. But it can take hours to ingest and then digest large prey. Warmer temperatures help the snake's digestion, so after a meal, it will find a sunny spot and relax.

BRAZILIAN WANDERING SPIDER

Why does this spider attack humans? Well, often it is minding its own business in a banana plant, when it is suddenly disturbed by farmworkers. Don't blame the spider—its natural response is to bite!

HERCULES BEETLE

This beetle spends more time as a larva than it does as an adult. The larva feeds on decaying wood for 12 to 18 months. The beetle then spends two to three months at rest in the pupal stage, and then only 8 to 12 months as a fully grown beetle.

GOLIATH TIGERFISH

Locals in the Congo say the tigerfish is the only fish that doesn't fear crocodiles, and that it actually eats smaller ones. However, fish are its staple diet. To catch them, it has evolved keen eyesight, and it is also able to pick up the vibrations emitted by other fish.

ELECTRIC EEL

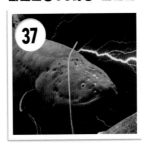

The eel's electricity works like a Taser, attacking the nervous system of its prey. The electric eel has one big advantage, though. It can deliver its shocks at 400 pulses per second, while a Taser sends out only 19 pulses per second.

HARPY EAGLE

Early South American explorers named these great birds after the harpies of ancient Greek mythology. They were ferocious half-women, half-bird monsters sent by the god Zeus to snatch people away from Earth—just as the harpy eagle snatches its prey from the rain forest.

LIFE IN THE TREETOPS

Poison dart frog can be very caring parents, with the male frog often tending to the eggs and newly hatched tadpoles. In some species, the dad climbs high up into the forest canopy, with the tadpoles piggybacking on him. He places the tadpoles in plants that hold pools of water. Bromeliads are perfect because they have cuplike flowers that catch water. One tadpole is placed in each pocket of water, probably so that predators will not be able to find them all. The tadpoles feed mainly on small insects in their treetop nursery—but Mom often adds to their diet by depositing her eggs into the water while Dad brings more water if their pools dry up.

DISGUISED AS A CHICK!

There are two other species of vampire bat besides the common vampire bat. They are the hairy-legged vampire bat and the white-winged vampire bat. These also live in Central and South America, and they feed on the blood of birds.

The white-winged vampire is very cunning. To feed on domestic chickens, it pretends to be a chick. It nuzzles up to a hen's brood patch—a featherless piece of skin on her underside that she uses to transfer heat to her eggs or chicks during nesting. The patch is packed with blood vessels. If the hen thinks it's her chick cuddling up, she'll sit on the bat, making it easy to drink from her!

FLAIL THEN FREEZE

The electric eel attacks and swallows fish so quickly it's impossible to see exactly what happens with the naked eye. In 2014, however, scientists used a high-speed camera that captures 1,000 frames per second to record an electric eel attacking a fish in a tank. It showed the eel using double or triple pulses to make the fish flail before the full high-frequency pulses made the fish freeze.

However, scientists are still not sure why the shocks don't electrocute the eel itself. The skin of the eel may be resistant to electricity. Or the eel's vital organs—the brain and the heart—may be insulated by fatty tissue. These organs are also located near the head, as far as possible from the electric cells lower down on the body.

ENTERING THE BELLY OF THE BEAST?

There are many films, books, and folktales about man-eating anacondas—but little evidence that they actually exist. In 2014 naturalist Paul Rosolie set out to test the truth of the stories. In a program called *Eaten Alive*, Rosolie volunteered to be the prey for a 20-foot (6-m) green anaconda while wearing an armored protective suit and helmet. The program didn't really live up to its billing. The anaconda took a nibble at Rosolie's helmet and gripped his arm, but then the stunt was called off because Rosolie was scared of breaking his arm. We'll just have to wait for another volunteer to see if the anaconda really will eat a human.

INDEX

THE AUTHOR

Matthew Rake lives in London, England, and has worked in publishing for more than twenty years. He has written on a wide variety of topics including science, sports, and the arts.

THE ARTIST

Award-winning illustrator Simon Mendez combines his love of nature and drawing by working as an illustrator with a focus on scientific and natural subjects. He paints on a wide variety of themes but mainly concentrates on portraits and animal subjects. He lives in the United Kingdom.

Picture Credits (abbreviations: t = top; b = bottom; c = center; l = left; r = right)

© www.shutterstock.com: 1c, 3c, 5br, 10l, 12l, 13tr, 14, 15tr, 16, 19tr, 23 tr, 27b, 28tr, 28cl, 28cr, 29tl, 29tr, 29b, 3-tr, 30bl.

25tr, Anaconda being held by Men: Vadim Petrakov / Shutterstock.com